the hope of
BELIEVE
easter

SELECTIONS FROM THE
NEW INTERNATIONAL VERSION

the hope of

BELIEVE

easter

GENERAL EDITOR
RANDY FRAZEE

ZONDERVAN®

ZONDERVAN
Believe: The Hope of Easter
Copyright © 2014 by Zondervan

Requests for information should be addressed to:
Zondervan, 3900 Sparks Drive SE, Grand Rapids, Michigan, 49546

Cover design: Extra Credit Projects

Printed in the United States of America

14 15 16 17 18 19 20 /OPM/ 10 9 8 7 6 5 4 3 2 1

Table of Contents

Foreword

> Praise be to the God and Father of our Lord Jesus
> Christ! In his great mercy he has given us new
> birth into a living hope through the resurrection of
> Jesus Christ from the dead, and into an inheritance
> that can never perish, spoil or fade.
> *1 Peter 1:3 – 4*

Maybe you're in a season of life where you've lost hope. A wise sage once told me, "You cannot cope without hope." It is impossible to deal with life's difficulties if there is no hope of a new and better day to come.

I have some good news. Easter is all about the celebration of the resurrection of Jesus Christ. Jesus rose from the dead to give us hope. This little book is aimed at helping you grab hold of it. It is a collection of Scripture stories from Genesis to Revelation built around three key themes of the Christian life — Beliefs, Practices and Virtues. All three hold the secret to God's offer of hope.

BELIEF — ETERNITY

To experience a brand of hope that never perishes, spoils or fades, you must come to understand and believe the unwavering promises God has made to us about the future. They are simply amazing.

PRACTICE — SINGLE-MINDEDNESS

For a belief to have a full impact on us, we can't just believe it in our heads; we must also believe it in our hearts. This spiritual practice will help the belief above take the 12-inch journey from the head to the heart.

VIRTUE — HOPE

As God's promises take root in your heart, hope will grow in you from the inside out.

Bask in the gift of God's Word this Easter and before long you will be declaring with confidence, "I can cope with the hope I have in Jesus Christ!"

— Randy Frazee
General Editor

CHAPTER

1

Eternity

---- KEY IDEA ----

I believe there is a heaven and a hell
and that Jesus will return to judge all people
and to establish his eternal kingdom.

---- KEY VERSE ----

Do not let your hearts be troubled. You believe in God;
believe also in me. My Father's house has many rooms;
if that were not so, would I have told you that
I am going there to prepare a place for you?
John 14:1 – 2

While the Old Testament writers don't address the afterlife in as much detail as the New Testament writers, the Old Testament does contain the magnificent description of the prophet Elijah being taken up to heaven without dying. Elijah is one of only three people taken to heaven in bodily form, the other two being Enoch (you can read about him in Genesis 5:21–24) and, of course, Jesus.

THE ENDING OF A LIFE

When the LORD was about to take Elijah up to heaven in a whirlwind, Elijah and Elisha were on their way from Gilgal. Elijah said to Elisha, "Stay here; the LORD has sent me to Bethel."

But Elisha said, "As surely as the LORD lives and as you live, I will not leave you." So they went down to Bethel.

The company of the prophets at Bethel came out to Elisha and asked, "Do you know that the LORD is going to take your master from you today?"

"Yes, I know," Elisha replied, "so be quiet."

Then Elijah said to him, "Stay here, Elisha; the LORD has sent me to Jericho."

And he replied, "As surely as the LORD lives and as you live, I will not leave you." So they went to Jericho.

The company of the prophets at Jericho went

up to Elisha and asked him, "Do you know that the LORD is going to take your master from you today?"

"Yes, I know," he replied, "so be quiet."

Then Elijah said to him, "Stay here; the LORD has sent me to the Jordan."

And he replied, "As surely as the LORD lives and as you live, I will not leave you." So the two of them walked on.

Fifty men from the company of the prophets went and stood at a distance, facing the place where Elijah and Elisha had stopped at the Jordan. Elijah took his cloak, rolled it up and struck the water with it. The water divided to the right and to the left, and the two of them crossed over on dry ground.

When they had crossed, Elijah said to Elisha, "Tell me, what can I do for you before I am taken from you?"

"Let me inherit a double portion of your spirit," Elisha replied.

"You have asked a difficult thing," Elijah said, "yet if you see me when I am taken from you, it will be yours — otherwise, it will not."

As they were walking along and talking together, suddenly a chariot of fire and horses of fire appeared and separated the two of them, and Elijah went up to heaven in a whirlwind. Elisha saw this and cried out, "My father! My father! The chariots and horsemen of Israel!" And Elisha saw him no more. Then he took hold of his garment and tore it in two.

Elisha then picked up Elijah's cloak that had fallen from him and went back and stood on the bank of the Jordan. He took the cloak that had fallen from Elijah and struck the water with it. "Where now is the LORD, the God of Elijah?" he asked. When he struck the water, it divided to the right and to the left, and he crossed over.

The company of the prophets from Jericho, who were watching, said, "The spirit of Elijah is resting on Elisha." And they went to meet him and bowed to the ground before him. "Look," they said, "we your servants have fifty able men. Let them go and look for your master. Perhaps the Spirit of the LORD has picked him up and set him down on some mountain or in some valley."

"No," Elisha replied, "do not send them."

But they persisted until he was too embarrassed to refuse. So he said, "Send them." And they sent fifty men, who searched for three days but did not find him. When they returned to Elisha, who was staying in Jericho, he said to them, "Didn't I tell you not to go?"

THE INTERMEDIATE STATE

What happens when we die? The New Testament indicates that people experience an "intermediate state," which refers to a person's existence between their time of death and the promised resurrection of their new body. Their earthly body goes into the grave; their spirit lives on in one of two places—in God's presence where they enjoy a time of peace until they receive their resurrected bodies or in a place of torment where they await final judgment. Jesus talked about this vividly in the story about a rich man and Lazarus (not the Lazarus Jesus raised from the dead). Jesus depicted the place of blessedness for the righteous as Abraham's side and the place of torment for the wicked as Hades.

"There was a rich man who was dressed in purple and fine linen and lived in luxury every day. At his gate was laid a beggar named Lazarus, covered with sores and longing to eat what fell from the rich man's table. Even the dogs came and licked his sores.

"The time came when the beggar died and the angels carried him to Abraham's side. The rich man also died and was buried. In Hades, where he was in torment, he looked up and saw Abraham far away, with Lazarus by his side. So he called to him, 'Father Abraham, have pity on me and send Lazarus to dip the tip of his finger in water and cool my tongue, because I am in agony in this fire.'

"But Abraham replied, 'Son, remember that

in your lifetime you received your good things, while Lazarus received bad things, but now he is comforted here and you are in agony. And besides all this, between us and you a great chasm has been set in place, so that those who want to go from here to you cannot, nor can anyone cross over from there to us.'

"He answered, 'Then I beg you, father, send Lazarus to my family, for I have five brothers. Let him warn them, so that they will not also come to this place of torment.'

"Abraham replied, 'They have Moses and the Prophets; let them listen to them.'

"'No, father Abraham,' he said, 'but if someone from the dead goes to them, they will repent.'

"He said to him, 'If they do not listen to Moses and the Prophets, they will not be convinced even if someone rises from the dead.'"

The Resurrection

The grand promise of God and the ultimate hope for all Christians is the resurrection. Just as Christ was raised from the dead and received an imperishable body, so will all those who believe in Christ. Paul, writing to the church at Corinth, details this major truth.

Now, brothers and sisters, I want to remind you of the gospel I preached to you, which you received and on which you have taken your stand. By this gospel you are saved, if you hold firmly to the word I preached to you. Otherwise, you have believed in vain.

For what I received I passed on to you as of first importance: that Christ died for our sins according to the Scriptures, that he was buried, that he was raised on the third day according to the Scriptures, and that he appeared to Cephas [Peter], and then to the Twelve. After that, he appeared to more than five hundred of the brothers and sisters at the same time, most of whom are still living, though some have fallen asleep. Then he appeared to James, then to all the apostles, and last of all he appeared to me also, as to one abnormally born.

For I am the least of the apostles and do not even deserve to be called an apostle, because I persecuted the church of God. But by the grace of God I am what I am, and his grace to me was not without effect. No, I worked harder than all of them — yet not I, but the grace of God that was with me. Whether, then, it is I or they, this is what we preach, and this is what you believed.

But if it is preached that Christ has been raised from the dead, how can some of you say that there is no resurrection of the dead? If there is no resurrection of the dead, then not even Christ has been raised. And if Christ has not been raised, our preaching is useless and so is your faith. More than that, we are then found to be false witnesses about God, for we have testified about God that he raised Christ from the dead. But he did not raise him if in fact the dead are not raised. For if the dead are not raised, then Christ has not been raised either. And if Christ has not been raised, your faith is futile; you are still in your sins. Then those also who have fallen asleep in Christ are lost. If only for this life we have hope in Christ, we are of all people most to be pitied.

But Christ has indeed been raised from the dead, the firstfruits of those who have fallen asleep. For since death came through a man, the resurrection of the dead comes also through a man. For as in Adam all die, so in Christ all will be made alive. But each in turn: Christ, the firstfruits; then, when he comes, those who belong to him. Then the end will come, when he hands over the kingdom to God the Father after he has destroyed all dominion, authority and power. For he must reign until he has put all his enemies under his feet. The last enemy to be destroyed is death. For he "has put everything under his feet." Now when it says that "everything" has been put under him, it is clear that this does not include God himself, who put everything under Christ. When he has done this, then the Son himself will be made subject to him who put everything under him, so that God may be all in all.

But someone will ask, "How are the dead raised? With what kind of body will they come?" How foolish! What you sow does not come to life unless it dies. When you sow, you do not plant the body that will be, but just a seed, perhaps of wheat or of something else. But God gives it a body as he has determined, and to each kind of seed he gives its own body. Not all flesh is the same: People have one kind of flesh, animals have another, birds another and fish another. There are also heavenly bodies and there are earthly bodies; but the splendor of the heavenly bodies is one kind, and the splendor of the earthly bodies is another. The sun has one kind of splendor, the moon another and the stars another; and star differs from star in splendor.

So will it be with the resurrection of the dead. The body that is sown is perishable, it is raised imperishable; it is sown in dishonor, it is raised in glory; it is sown in weakness, it is raised in power; it is sown a natural body, it is raised a spiritual body.

If there is a natural body, there is also a spiritual body. So it is written: "The first man Adam became a living being"; the last Adam, a life-giving spirit. The spiritual did not come first, but the natural, and after that the spiritual. The first man was of the dust of the earth; the second man is of heaven. As was the earthly man, so are those who are of the earth; and as is the heavenly man, so also are those who are of heaven. And just as we have borne the image of the earthly man, so shall we bear the image of the heavenly man.

I declare to you, brothers and sisters, that flesh and blood cannot inherit the kingdom of God, nor does the perishable inherit the imperishable. Listen, I tell you a mystery: We will not all sleep, but we will all be changed — in a flash, in the twinkling of an eye, at the last trumpet. For the trumpet will sound, the dead will be raised imperishable, and we will be changed. For the perishable must clothe itself with the imperishable, and the mortal with immortality. When the perishable has been clothed with the imperishable, and the mortal with immortality, then the saying that is written will come true: "Death has been swallowed up in victory."

"Where, O death, is your victory?
Where, O death, is your sting?"

The sting of death is sin, and the power of sin is the law. But thanks be to God! He gives us the victory through our Lord Jesus Christ.

Therefore, my dear brothers and sisters, stand firm. Let nothing move you. Always give yourselves fully to the work of the Lord, because you know that your labor in the Lord is not in vain.

It is written: "I believed; therefore I have spoken." Since we have that same spirit of faith, we also believe and therefore speak, because we know that the one who raised the Lord Jesus from the dead will also raise us with Jesus and present us with you to himself. All this is for your benefit, so that the grace that is reaching more and more people may cause thanksgiving to overflow to the glory of God.

Therefore we do not lose heart. Though outwardly we are wasting away, yet inwardly we are being renewed day by day. For our light and momentary troubles are achieving for us an eternal glory that far outweighs them all. So we fix our eyes not on what is seen, but on what is unseen, since what is seen is temporary, but what is unseen is eternal.

For we know that if the earthly tent we live in is destroyed, we have a building from God, an eternal house in heaven, not built by human hands. Meanwhile we groan, longing to be clothed instead with our heavenly dwelling, because when we are clothed, we will not be found naked. For while we are in this tent, we groan and are burdened, because we do not wish to be unclothed but to be clothed instead with our heavenly dwelling, so that what is mortal may be swallowed up by life. Now the one who has fashioned us for this very purpose is God, who has given us the Spirit as a deposit, guaranteeing what is to come.

Therefore we are always confident and know that as long as we are at home in the body we are away from the Lord. For we live by faith, not by sight. We are confident, I say, and would prefer to be away from the body and at home with the Lord. So we make it our goal to please him, whether we are at home in the body or away from it. For we must all appear before the judgment seat of Christ, so that each of us may receive what is due us for the things done while in the body, whether good or bad.

THE RETURN OF CHRIST

The event that will trigger this promised resurrection is the second coming of Christ. There are varied beliefs about the details leading up to this grand occasion, but all followers of Jesus embrace its truth and significance. Often the Bible refers to the return of Christ as the "day of the Lord." Paul uses this phrase in an important letter addressed to the church at Thessalonica. Some of the believers there thought all Christians would be alive at the return of Christ, causing them to be concerned about fellow believers who had died. Paul explains that on the great day of Christ's return God will resurrect those who have died and then all believers

*will be brought together and will be with the
Lord Jesus forever.*

Brothers and sisters, we do not want you to be
uninformed about those who sleep in death, so
that you do not grieve like the rest of mankind,
who have no hope. For we believe that Jesus died
and rose again, and so we believe that God will
bring with Jesus those who have fallen asleep in
him. According to the Lord's word, we tell you
that we who are still alive, who are left until the
coming of the Lord, will certainly not precede
those who have fallen asleep. For the Lord himself
will come down from heaven, with a loud command, with the voice of the archangel and with
the trumpet call of God, and the dead in Christ
will rise first. After that, we who are still alive and
are left will be caught up together with them in
the clouds to meet the Lord in the air. And so we
will be with the Lord forever. Therefore encourage one another with these words.

Now, brothers and sisters, about times and
dates we do not need to write to you, for you know
very well that the day of the Lord will come like a
thief in the night. While people are saying, "Peace
and safety," destruction will come on them suddenly, as labor pains on a pregnant woman, and
they will not escape.

But you, brothers and sisters, are not in darkness so that this day should surprise you like a thief. You are all children of the light and children of the day. We do not belong to the night or to the darkness. So then, let us not be like others, who are asleep, but let us be awake and sober. For those who sleep, sleep at night, and those who get drunk, get drunk at night. But since we belong to the day, let us be sober, putting on faith and love as a breastplate, and the hope of salvation as a helmet. For God did not appoint us to suffer wrath but to receive salvation through our Lord Jesus Christ. He died for us so that, whether we are awake or asleep, we may live together with him. Therefore encourage one another and build each other up, just as in fact you are doing.

The apostle Peter also writes in great detail about "the day of the Lord," adding further clarification and admonition regarding how believers should live their lives in light of this future reality.

Dear friends, this is now my second letter to you. I have written both of them as reminders to stimulate you to wholesome thinking. I want you to recall the words spoken in the past by the holy prophets and the command given by our Lord and Savior through your apostles.

Above all, you must understand that in the last days scoffers will come, scoffing and following their own evil desires. They will say, "Where is this 'coming' he promised? Ever since our ancestors died, everything goes on as it has since the beginning of creation." But they deliberately forget that long ago by God's word the heavens came into being and the earth was formed out of water and by water. By these waters also the world of that time was deluged and destroyed. By the same word the present heavens and earth are reserved for fire, being kept for the day of judgment and destruction of the ungodly.

But do not forget this one thing, dear friends: With the Lord a day is like a thousand years, and a thousand years are like a day. The Lord is not slow in keeping his promise, as some understand slowness. Instead he is patient with you, not wanting anyone to perish, but everyone to come to repentance.

But the day of the Lord will come like a thief. The heavens will disappear with a roar; the elements will be destroyed by fire, and the earth and everything done in it will be laid bare.

Since everything will be destroyed in this way, what kind of people ought you to be? You ought to live holy and godly lives as you look forward to the day of God and speed its coming. That day will bring about the destruction of the heavens by fire, and the elements will melt in the heat. But in keeping with his promise we are looking forward to a new heaven and a new earth, where righteousness dwells.

So then, dear friends, since you are looking forward to this, make every effort to be found spotless, blameless and at peace with him. Bear in mind that our Lord's patience means salvation, just as our dear brother Paul also wrote you with the wisdom that God gave him. He writes the same way in all his letters, speaking in them of these matters. His letters contain some things that are hard to understand, which ignorant and unstable people distort, as they do the other Scriptures, to their own destruction.

Therefore, dear friends, since you have been forewarned, be on your guard so that you may not be carried away by the error of the lawless and fall from your secure position. But grow in the grace and knowledge of our Lord and Savior Jesus Christ. To him be glory both now and forever! Amen.

NEW HEAVEN AND NEW EARTH

After Jesus returns and we are resurrected into our imperishable bodies, there will be a final judgment by God of every nation. John saw and recorded a vision from God about what will happen at this time of judgment. John wrote down the final movement in God's grand story — the restoration of what was lost in the beginning.

What we read in the opening creation story of Genesis we see again in Revelation—a re-creation—but on a grander scale to accommodate all the people over the centuries who have embraced Christ and received eternal life.

I saw a great white throne and him who was seated on it. The earth and the heavens fled from his presence, and there was no place for them. And I saw the dead, great and small, standing before the throne, and books were opened. Another book was opened, which is the book of life. The dead were judged according to what they had done as recorded in the books. The sea gave up the dead that were in it, and death and Hades gave up the dead that were in them, and each person was judged according to what they had done. Then death and Hades were thrown into the lake of fire. The lake of fire is the second death. Anyone whose name was not found written in the book of life was thrown into the lake of fire.

Then I saw "a new heaven and a new earth," for the first heaven and the first earth had passed away, and there was no longer any sea. I saw the Holy City, the new Jerusalem, coming down out of heaven from God, prepared as a bride beautifully dressed for her husband. And I heard a loud voice from the throne saying, "Look! God's dwelling place is now among the people, and he will dwell with them. They will be his people, and God himself will be with them and be their God. 'He will wipe every tear from their eyes. There will be no more death' or mourning or crying or pain, for the old order of things has passed away."

He who was seated on the throne said, "I am making everything new!" Then he said, "Write this down, for these words are trustworthy and true."

He said to me: "It is done. I am the Alpha and the Omega, the Beginning and the End. To the thirsty I will give water without cost from the spring of the water of life. Those who are victorious will inherit all this, and I will be their God and they will be my children. But the cowardly, the unbelieving, the vile, the murderers, the sexually immoral, those who practice magic arts, the idolaters and all liars — they will be consigned to the fiery lake of burning sulfur. This is the second death."

One of the seven angels who had the seven bowls full of the seven last plagues came and said to me, "Come, I will show you the bride, the wife of the Lamb." And he carried me away in the Spirit to a mountain great and high, and showed me the Holy City, Jerusalem, coming down out of heaven from God. It shone with the glory of God, and its brilliance was like that of a very precious jewel, like a jasper, clear as crystal. It had a great, high

wall with twelve gates, and with twelve angels at
the gates. On the gates were written the names of
the twelve tribes of Israel. There were three gates
on the east, three on the north, three on the south
and three on the west. The wall of the city had
twelve foundations, and on them were the names
of the twelve apostles of the Lamb.

The angel who talked with me had a measur-
ing rod of gold to measure the city, its gates and
its walls. The city was laid out like a square, as
long as it was wide. He measured the city with the
rod and found it to be 12,000 stadia in length, and
as wide and high as it is long. The angel measured
the wall using human measurement, and it was
144 cubits thick. The wall was made of jasper, and
the city of pure gold, as pure as glass. The foundations of the city walls were decorated with every kind of precious stone. The first foundation
was jasper, the second sapphire, the third agate,
the fourth emerald, the fifth onyx, the sixth ruby,
the seventh chrysolite, the eighth beryl, the ninth
topaz, the tenth turquoise, the eleventh jacinth,
and the twelfth amethyst. The twelve gates were
twelve pearls, each gate made of a single pearl.
The great street of the city was of gold, as pure as
transparent glass.

I did not see a temple in the city, because the
Lord God Almighty and the Lamb are its temple.
The city does not need the sun or the moon to

shine on it, for the glory of God gives it light, and the Lamb is its lamp. The nations will walk by its light, and the kings of the earth will bring their splendor into it. On no day will its gates ever be shut, for there will be no night there. The glory and honor of the nations will be brought into it. Nothing impure will ever enter it, nor will anyone who does what is shameful or deceitful, but only those whose names are written in the Lamb's book of life.

Then the angel showed me the river of the water of life, as clear as crystal, flowing from the throne of God and of the Lamb down the middle of the great street of the city. On each side of the river stood the tree of life, bearing twelve crops of fruit, yielding its fruit every month. And the leaves of the tree are for the healing of the nations. No longer will there be any curse. The throne of God and of the Lamb will be in the city, and his servants will serve him. They will see his face, and his name will be on their foreheads. There will be no more night. They will not need the light of a lamp or the light of the sun, for the Lord God will give them light. And they will reign for ever and ever.

The angel said to me, "These words are trustworthy and true. The Lord, the God who inspires the prophets, sent his angel to show his servants the things that must soon take place."

"Look, I am coming soon! Blessed is the one who keeps the words of the prophecy written in this scroll."

I, John, am the one who heard and saw these things. And when I had heard and seen them, I fell down to worship at the feet of the angel who had been showing them to me. But he said to me, "Don't do that! I am a fellow servant with you and with your fellow prophets and with all who keep the words of this scroll. Worship God!"

Then he told me, "Do not seal up the words of the prophecy of this scroll, because the time is near. Let the one who does wrong continue to do wrong; let the vile person continue to be vile; let the one who does right continue to do right; and let the holy person continue to be holy."

"Look, I am coming soon! My reward is with me, and I will give to each person according to what they have done. I am the Alpha and the Omega, the First and the Last, the Beginning and the End.

"Blessed are those who wash their robes, that they may have the right to the tree of life and may go through the gates into the city. Outside are the dogs, those who practice magic arts, the sexually immoral, the murderers, the idolaters and everyone who loves and practices falsehood.

"I, Jesus, have sent my angel to give you this

testimony for the churches. I am the Root and the Offspring of David, and the bright Morning Star."

The Spirit and the bride say, "Come!" And let the one who hears say, "Come!" Let the one who is thirsty come; and let the one who wishes take the free gift of the water of life.

I warn everyone who hears the words of the prophecy of this scroll: If anyone adds anything to them, God will add to that person the plagues described in this scroll. And if anyone takes words away from this scroll of prophecy, God will take away from that person any share in the tree of life and in the Holy City, which are described in this scroll.

He who testifies to these things says, "Yes, I am coming soon."

Amen. Come, Lord Jesus.

The grace of the Lord Jesus be with God's people. Amen.

In Jesus' last week on earth before he returned to the Father, he comforted the disciples concerning the future. He informed them that he was leaving, but he also promised that he would be overseeing the construction of a place for each of them in heaven — the New Jerusalem John saw and described. As you read these words, please know that Jesus' message to the

*disciples applies to you as well. He has prepared
an eternal home for all those who believe.*

"Do not let your hearts be troubled. You believe in God; believe also in me. My Father's house
has many rooms; if that were not so, would I have
told you that I am going there to prepare a place
for you? And if I go and prepare a place for you, I
will come back and take you to be with me that
you also may be where I am. You know the way to
the place where I am going."

Thomas said to him, "Lord, we don't know
where you are going, so how can we know the
way?"

Jesus answered, "I am the way and the truth
and the life. No one comes to the Father except
through me. If you really know me, you will know
my Father as well. From now on, you do know
him and have seen him."

CHAPTER

2

Single-Mindedness

--- KEY IDEA ---

I focus on God and his priorities for my life.

--- KEY VERSE ---

But seek first his kingdom and his righteousness,
and all these things will be given to you as well.
Matthew 6:33

*To be single-minded means to have one desire
that trumps all others. One goal. One focus.
From the beginning God made clear what his
people's main focus should be—him.*

PRINCIPLES OF SINGLE-MINDEDNESS

"I am the LORD your God, who brought you
out of Egypt, out of the land of slavery. You shall
have no other gods before me."

*In the first of the Ten Commandments, God
commanded the Israelites to serve him exclu-
sively because he was worthy of their trust, as
he had proved by delivering them from Egypt.
Later, just before Moses died and the Israelites entered the promised land, God inspired
Moses to remind the people of their single-
minded calling.*

These are the commands, decrees and laws
the LORD your God directed me to teach you to
observe in the land that you are crossing the Jordan to possess, so that you, your children and
their children after them may fear the LORD your
God as long as you live by keeping all his decrees
and commands that I give you, and so that you
may enjoy long life. Hear, Israel, and be careful to
obey so that it may go well with you and that you
may increase greatly in a land flowing with milk

and honey, just as the LORD, the God of your ancestors, promised you.

Hear, O Israel: The LORD our God, the LORD
is one. Love the LORD your God with all your
heart and with all your soul and with all your
strength. These commandments that I give you
today are to be on your hearts. Impress them on
your children. Talk about them when you sit at
home and when you walk along the road, when
you lie down and when you get up. Tie them as
symbols on your hands and bind them on your
foreheads. Write them on the doorframes of your
houses and on your gates.

*God's people needed to submit fully to his
authority and believe he could provide all they
needed. It's this kind of trust that Jesus calls us
to demonstrate as his disciples.*

"Do not store up for yourselves treasures on
earth, where moths and vermin destroy, and
where thieves break in and steal. But store up for
yourselves treasures in heaven, where moths and
vermin do not destroy, and where thieves do not
break in and steal. For where your treasure is,
there your heart will be also.

"The eye is the lamp of the body. If your eyes
are healthy, your whole body will be full of light.
But if your eyes are unhealthy, your whole body

will be full of darkness. If then the light within you is darkness, how great is that darkness!

"No one can serve two masters. Either you will hate the one and love the other, or you will be devoted to the one and despise the other. You cannot serve both God and money.

"Therefore I tell you, do not worry about your life, what you will eat or drink; or about your body, what you will wear. Is not life more than food, and the body more than clothes? Look at the birds of the air; they do not sow or reap or store away in barns, and yet your heavenly Father feeds them. Are you not much more valuable than they? Can any one of you by worrying add a single hour to your life?

"And why do you worry about clothes? See how the flowers of the field grow. They do not labor or spin. Yet I tell you that not even Solomon in all his splendor was dressed like one of these. If that is how God clothes the grass of the field, which is here today and tomorrow is thrown into the fire, will he not much more clothe you — you of little faith? So do not worry, saying, 'What shall we eat?' or 'What shall we drink?' or 'What shall we wear?' For the pagans run after all these things, and your heavenly Father knows that you need them. But seek first his kingdom and his righteousness, and all these things will be given to you as well."

During the first century, the apostle Paul trav-
eled from city to city teaching people about the
gift of salvation through Jesus and how believ-
ers could single-mindedly follow Christ. In many
cases, a combative group of religious leaders
approached the new churches after Paul left and
tried to undermine his authority and teaching.
They boasted about their religious credentials
and weighed down Paul's message with Jew-
ish laws and traditions. This infuriated Paul, who
then urged the believers to follow his example
in keeping their focus steadfastly on Jesus.

Further, my brothers and sisters, rejoice in the
Lord! It is no trouble for me to write the same
things to you again, and it is a safeguard for you.
Watch out for those dogs, those evildoers, those
mutilators of the flesh. For it is we who are the
circumcision, we who serve God by his Spirit,
who boast in Christ Jesus, and who put no confidence in the flesh — though I myself have reasons
for such confidence.

If someone else thinks they have reasons to
put confidence in the flesh, I have more: circum-
cised on the eighth day, of the people of Israel, of
the tribe of Benjamin, a Hebrew of Hebrews; in
regard to the law, a Pharisee; as for zeal, persecut-
ing the church; as for righteousness based on the
law, faultless.

But whatever were gains to me I now consider loss for the sake of Christ. What is more, I consider everything a loss because of the surpassing worth of knowing Christ Jesus my Lord, for whose sake I have lost all things. I consider them garbage, that I may gain Christ and be found in him, not having a righteousness of my own that comes from the law, but that which is through faith in Christ — the righteousness that comes from God on the basis of faith. I want to know Christ — yes, to know the power of his resurrection and participation in his sufferings, becoming like him in his death, and so, somehow, attaining to the resurrection from the dead.

Not that I have already obtained all this, or have already arrived at my goal, but I press on to take hold of that for which Christ Jesus took hold of me. Brothers and sisters, I do not consider myself yet to have taken hold of it. But one thing I do: Forgetting what is behind and straining toward what is ahead, I press on toward the goal to win the prize for which God has called me heavenward in Christ Jesus.

PROFILES OF SINGLE-MINDEDNESS

King Jehoshaphat of the southern kingdom of Judah faced a tremendous challenge. His land was threatened by a hostile army. Rather than being overcome by fear, Jehoshaphat led the

people to turn to the Lord in single-minded and
wholehearted trust.

The Moabites and Ammonites with some of
the Meunites came to wage war against Jehoshaphat.

Some people came and told Jehoshaphat, "A
vast army is coming against you from Edom,
from the other side of the Dead Sea. It is already
in Hazezon Tamar" (that is, En Gedi). Alarmed,
Jehoshaphat resolved to inquire of the LORD, and
he proclaimed a fast for all Judah. The people of
Judah came together to seek help from the LORD;
indeed, they came from every town in Judah to
seek him.

Then Jehoshaphat stood up in the assembly of
Judah and Jerusalem at the temple of the LORD in
the front of the new courtyard and said:

"LORD, the God of our ancestors, are you not
the God who is in heaven? You rule over all the
kingdoms of the nations. Power and might are in
your hand, and no one can withstand you. Our
God, did you not drive out the inhabitants of this
land before your people Israel and give it forever
to the descendants of Abraham your friend? They
have lived in it and have built in it a sanctuary
for your Name, saying, 'If calamity comes upon
us, whether the sword of judgment, or plague or

famine, we will stand in your presence before this temple that bears your Name and will cry out to you in our distress, and you will hear us and save us.'

"But now here are men from Ammon, Moab and Mount Seir, whose territory you would not allow Israel to invade when they came from Egypt; so they turned away from them and did not destroy them. See how they are repaying us by coming to drive us out of the possession you gave us as an inheritance. Our God, will you not judge them? For we have no power to face this vast army that is attacking us. We do not know what to do, but our eyes are on you."

All the men of Judah, with their wives and children and little ones, stood there before the LORD.

Then the Spirit of the LORD came on Jahaziel son of Zechariah, the son of Benaiah, the son of Jeiel, the son of Mattaniah, a Levite and descendant of Asaph, as he stood in the assembly.

He said: "Listen, King Jehoshaphat and all who live in Judah and Jerusalem! This is what the LORD says to you: 'Do not be afraid or discouraged because of this vast army. For the battle is not yours, but God's. Tomorrow march down against them. They will be climbing up by the Pass of Ziz, and you will find them at the end of the gorge in the Desert of Jeruel. You will not have to fight this battle. Take up your positions; stand firm and see the deliverance the LORD will give you, Judah and Jerusalem. Do not be afraid; do not be discouraged. Go out to face them tomorrow, and the LORD will be with you.'"

Jehoshaphat bowed down with his face to the ground, and all the people of Judah and Jerusalem fell down in worship before the LORD. Then some Levites from the Kohathites and Korahites stood up and praised the LORD, the God of Israel, with a very loud voice.

Early in the morning they left for the Desert of Tekoa. As they set out, Jehoshaphat stood and said, "Listen to me, Judah and people of Jerusalem! Have faith in the LORD your God and you will be upheld; have faith in his prophets and you will be successful." After consulting the people, Jehoshaphat appointed men to sing to the LORD and to praise him for the splendor of his holiness as they went out at the head of the army, saying:

"Give thanks to the LORD,
    for his love endures forever."

As they began to sing and praise, the LORD set ambushes against the men of Ammon and Moab and Mount Seir who were invading Judah, and they were defeated. The Ammonites and Moabites rose up against the men from Mount Seir to destroy and annihilate them. After they finished slaughtering the men from Seir, they helped to destroy one another.

When the men of Judah came to the place that overlooks the desert and looked toward the vast army, they saw only dead bodies lying on the ground; no one had escaped. So Jehoshaphat and his men went to carry off their plunder, and they found among them a great amount of equipment and clothing and also articles of value — more than they could take away. There was so much plunder that it took three days to collect it. On the fourth day they assembled in the Valley of Berakah, where they praised the LORD. This is why it is called the Valley of Berakah to this day.

Then, led by Jehoshaphat, all the men of Judah and Jerusalem returned joyfully to Jerusalem, for the LORD had given them cause to rejoice over their enemies. They entered Jerusalem and went to the temple of the LORD with harps and lyres and trumpets.

The fear of God came on all the surrounding kingdoms when they heard how the LORD had fought against the enemies of Israel. And the kingdom of Jehoshaphat was at peace, for his God had given him rest on every side.

While Jehoshaphat certainly proved that his focus was on God, Jesus serves as the exemplary model for the type of single-mindedness God had in mind when he announced in the first of his Ten Commandments: "You shall have no other gods before me." Living out those ancient rules, Jesus didn't make choices based on his desires or anyone else's expectations. His sole goal was to live according to his Father's will.

When Jesus spoke again to the people, he said, "I am the light of the world. Whoever follows me will never walk in darkness, but will have the light of life."

The Pharisees challenged him, "Here you are, appearing as your own witness; your testimony is not valid."

Jesus answered, "Even if I testify on my own behalf, my testimony is valid, for I know where I came from and where I am going. But you have no idea where I come from or where I am going. You judge by human standards; I pass judgment on no one. But if I do judge, my decisions are true, because I am not alone. I stand with the Father, who sent me. In your own Law it is written that the testimony of two witnesses is true. I am one who testifies for myself; my other witness is the Father, who sent me."

Then they asked him, "Where is your father?"

"You do not know me or my Father," Jesus replied. "If you knew me, you would know my

Father also." He spoke these words while teaching in the temple courts near the place where the offerings were put. Yet no one seized him, because his hour had not yet come.

Once more Jesus said to them, "I am going away, and you will look for me, and you will die in your sin. Where I go, you cannot come."

This made the Jews ask, "Will he kill himself? Is that why he says, 'Where I go, you cannot come'?"

But he continued, "You are from below; I am from above. You are of this world; I am not of this world. I told you that you would die in your sins; if you do not believe that I am he, you will indeed die in your sins."

"Who are you?" they asked.

"Just what I have been telling you from the beginning," Jesus replied. "I have much to say in judgment of you. But he who sent me is trustworthy, and what I have heard from him I tell the world."

They did not understand that he was telling them about his Father. So Jesus said, "When you have lifted up the Son of Man, then you will know that I am he and that I do nothing on my own but speak just what the Father has taught me. The one who sent me is with me; he has not left me alone, for I always do what pleases him." Even as he spoke, many believed in him.

Unfortunately, Jesus' disciple Peter had a bit more trouble retaining his single-minded focus when he was met with distraction. Peter's experience is a good reminder of how we are to think about Jesus, and keep our eyes on him, even when our thoughts get sidetracked or we feel frightened.

Jesus made the disciples get into the boat and go on ahead of him to the other side, while he dismissed the crowd. After he had dismissed them, he went up on a mountainside by himself to pray. Later that night, he was there alone, and the boat was already a considerable distance from land, buffeted by the waves because the wind was against it.

Shortly before dawn Jesus went out to them, walking on the lake. When the disciples saw him walking on the lake, they were terrified. "It's a ghost," they said, and cried out in fear.

But Jesus immediately said to them: "Take courage! It is I. Don't be afraid."

"Lord, if it's you," Peter replied, "tell me to come to you on the water."

"Come," he said.

Then Peter got down out of the boat, walked on the water and came toward Jesus. But when he saw the wind, he was afraid and, beginning to sink, cried out, "Lord, save me!"

Immediately Jesus reached out his hand and caught him. "You of little faith," he said, "why did you doubt?"

And when they climbed into the boat, the wind died down. Then those who were in the boat worshiped him, saying, "Truly you are the Son of God."

When they had crossed over, they landed at Gennesaret. And when the men of that place recognized Jesus, they sent word to all the surrounding country. People brought all their sick to him and begged him to let the sick just touch the edge of his cloak, and all who touched it were healed.

Ultimately, the disciples adopted Jesus' bold and unwavering devotion to God and his purposes.

The apostles performed many signs and wonders among the people. And all the believers used to meet together in Solomon's Colonnade. No one else dared join them, even though they were highly regarded by the people. Nevertheless, more and more men and women believed in the Lord and were added to their number. As a result, people brought the sick into the streets and laid them on beds and mats so that at least Peter's shadow might fall on some of them as he passed by. Crowds gathered also from the towns around

Jerusalem, bringing their sick and those tormented by impure spirits, and all of them were healed.

Then the high priest and all his associates, who were members of the party of the Sadducees, were filled with jealousy. They arrested the apostles and put them in the public jail. But during the night an angel of the Lord opened the doors of the jail and brought them out. "Go, stand in the temple courts," he said, "and tell the people all about this new life."

At daybreak they entered the temple courts, as they had been told, and began to teach the people.

When the high priest and his associates arrived, they called together the Sanhedrin — the full assembly of the elders of Israel — and sent to the jail for the apostles. But on arriving at the jail, the officers did not find them there. So they went back and reported, "We found the jail securely locked, with the guards standing at the doors; but when we opened them, we found no one inside." On hearing this report, the captain of the temple guard and the chief priests were at a loss, wondering what this might lead to.

Then someone came and said, "Look! The men you put in jail are standing in the temple courts teaching the people." At that, the captain went with his officers and brought the apostles. They did not use force, because they feared that the people would stone them.

The apostles were brought in and made to appear before the Sanhedrin to be questioned by the high priest. "We gave you strict orders not to teach in this name," he said. "Yet you have filled Jerusalem with your teaching and are determined to make us guilty of this man's blood."

Peter and the other apostles replied: "We must obey God rather than human beings! The God of our ancestors raised Jesus from the dead — whom you killed by hanging him on a cross. God exalted him to his own right hand as Prince and Savior that he might bring Israel to repentance and forgive their sins. We are witnesses of these things, and so is the Holy Spirit, whom God has given to those who obey him."

When they heard this, they were furious and wanted to put them to death. But a Pharisee named Gamaliel, a teacher of the law, who was honored by all the people, stood up in the Sanhedrin and ordered that the men be put outside for a little while. Then he addressed the Sanhedrin: "Men of Israel, consider carefully what you intend to do to these men. Some time ago Theudas appeared, claiming to be somebody, and about four hundred men rallied to him. He was killed, all his followers were dispersed, and it all came to nothing. After him, Judas the Galilean appeared in the days of the census and led a band of people in revolt. He too was killed, and all his followers were scattered. Therefore, in the present case I advise you: Leave these men alone! Let them go! For if their purpose or activity is of human origin, it will fail. But if it is from God, you will not be able to stop these men; you will only find yourselves fighting against God."

His speech persuaded them. They called the apostles in and had them flogged. Then they ordered them not to speak in the name of Jesus, and let them go.

The apostles left the Sanhedrin, rejoicing because they had been counted worthy of suffering disgrace for the Name. Day after day, in the temple courts and from house to house, they never stopped teaching and proclaiming the good news that Jesus is the Messiah.

PRODUCT OF SINGLE-MINDEDNESS

Near the end of the book of Deuteronomy— and Moses' life—the Lord called the Israelites to make a choice: Trust and obey his commands or go their own way. Speaking through Moses, God gave this message to his people. And what was the result of the people's decision? Because they chose obedience, the following seven years were the most fruitful years in Israel's history—the Glory Days!

You yourselves know how we lived in Egypt and how we passed through the countries on the way here. You saw among them their detestable images and idols of wood and stone, of silver and gold. Make sure there is no man or woman, clan or tribe among you today whose heart turns away from the LORD our God to go and worship the gods of those nations; make sure there is no root among you that produces such bitter poison.

When such a person hears the words of this oath and they invoke a blessing on themselves, thinking, "I will be safe, even though I persist in going my own way," they will bring disaster on the watered land as well as the dry. The LORD will never be willing to forgive them; his wrath and zeal will burn against them. All the curses written in this book will fall on them, and the LORD will blot out their names from under heaven. The LORD will single them out from all the tribes of Israel for disaster, according to all the curses of the covenant written in this Book of the Law.

Your children who follow you in later generations and foreigners who come from distant lands will see the calamities that have fallen on the land and the diseases with which the LORD has afflicted it. The whole land will be a burning waste of salt and sulfur — nothing planted, nothing sprouting, no vegetation growing on it. It will be like the destruction of Sodom and Gomorrah,

Admah and Zeboyim, which the LORD overthrew in fierce anger. All the nations will ask: "Why has the LORD done this to this land? Why this fierce, burning anger?"

And the answer will be: "It is because this people abandoned the covenant of the LORD, the God of their ancestors, the covenant he made with them when he brought them out of Egypt. They went off and worshiped other gods and bowed down to them, gods they did not know, gods he had not given them. Therefore the LORD's anger burned against this land, so that he brought on it all the curses written in this book. In furious anger and in great wrath the LORD uprooted them from their land and thrust them into another land, as it is now."

The secret things belong to the LORD our God, but the things revealed belong to us and to our children forever, that we may follow all the words of this law.

When all these blessings and curses I have set before you come on you and you take them to heart wherever the LORD your God disperses you among the nations, and when you and your children return to the LORD your God and obey him with all your heart and with all your soul according to everything I command you today, then the LORD your God will restore your fortunes and have compassion on you and gather you again from all the nations where he scattered you. Even if you have been banished to the most distant land under the heavens, from there the LORD your God will gather you and bring you back. He will bring you to the land that belonged to your ancestors, and you will take possession of it. He will make you more prosperous and numerous than your ancestors. The LORD your God will circumcise your hearts and the hearts of your descendants, so that you may love him with all your heart and with all your soul, and live. The LORD your God will put all these curses on your enemies who hate and persecute you. You will again obey the LORD and follow all his commands I am giving you today. Then the LORD your God will make you most prosperous in all the work of your hands and in the fruit of your womb, the young of your livestock and the crops of your land. The LORD will again delight in you and make you prosperous, just as he delighted in your ancestors, if you obey the LORD your God and keep his commands and decrees that are written in this Book of the Law and turn to the LORD your God with all your heart and with all your soul.

Now what I am commanding you today is not too difficult for you or beyond your reach. It is not up in heaven, so that you have to ask, "Who will ascend into heaven to get it and proclaim it to us so we may obey it?" Nor is it beyond the sea, so that you have to ask, "Who will cross the sea to get it and proclaim it to us so we may obey it?" No, the word is very near you; it is in your mouth and in your heart so you may obey it.

See, I set before you today life and prosperity, death and destruction. For I command you today to love the LORD your God, to walk in obedience to him, and to keep his commands, decrees and laws; then you will live and increase, and the LORD your God will bless you in the land you are entering to possess.

But if your heart turns away and you are not obedient, and if you are drawn away to bow down to other gods and worship them, I declare to you this day that you will certainly be destroyed. You will not live long in the land you are crossing the Jordan to enter and possess.

This day I call the heavens and the earth as witnesses against you that I have set before you life and death, blessings and curses. Now choose life, so that you and your children may live and that you may love the LORD your God, listen to his voice, and hold fast to him. For the LORD is your life, and he will give you many years in the land he swore to give to your fathers, Abraham, Isaac and Jacob.

In the New Testament, the apostle Paul also challenged believers to a single-minded com-

mitment to God. And with his exhortations came encouraging promises about the fruitful results of such devotion. As with Israel, so with us today: If we single-mindedly focus on Christ and his priorities for our lives, we will experience our Glory Days!

Therefore, I urge you, brothers and sisters, in view of God's mercy, to offer your bodies as a living sacrifice, holy and pleasing to God — this is your true and proper worship. Do not conform to the pattern of this world, but be transformed by the renewing of your mind. Then you will be able to test and approve what God's will is — his good, pleasing and perfect will.

Since, then, you have been raised with Christ, set your hearts on things above, where Christ is, seated at the right hand of God. Set your minds on things above, not on earthly things. For you died, and your life is now hidden with Christ in God. When Christ, who is your life, appears, then you also will appear with him in glory.

Let the peace of Christ rule in your hearts, since as members of one body you were called to peace. And be thankful. Let the message of Christ dwell among you richly as you teach and admonish one another with all wisdom through psalms, hymns, and songs from the Spirit, singing to God with gratitude in your hearts. And whatever you do, whether in word or deed, do it all in the name of the Lord Jesus, giving thanks to God the Father through him.

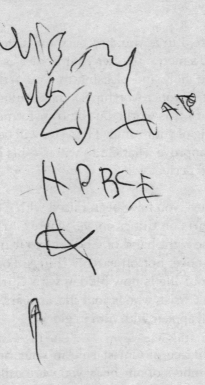

CHAPTER

3

Hope

———— KEY IDEA ————

I can cope with the hardships of life
because of the hope I have in Jesus Christ.

———— KEY VERSE ————

We have this hope as an anchor for the soul,
firm and secure. It enters the inner sanctuary
behind the curtain, where our forerunner,
Jesus, has entered on our behalf.
Hebrews 6:19–20

THE NEED FOR HOPE

It is impossible to cope without hope. Job had lost everything and was running out of strength. He wanted to die. His "friends" came to comfort him. His response to his unhelpful friends is the expression of a man without hope.

Job replied:

> "If only my anguish could be weighed
>   and all my misery be placed on the
>   scales!
> It would surely outweigh the sand of the
>   seas —
>   no wonder my words have been
>   impetuous.
> The arrows of the Almighty are in me,
>   my spirit drinks in their poison;
>   God's terrors are marshaled against me.
> Does a wild donkey bray when it has
>   grass,
>   or an ox bellow when it has fodder?
> Is tasteless food eaten without salt,
>   or is there flavor in the sap of the
>   mallow?
> I refuse to touch it;
>   such food makes me ill.

> "Oh, that I might have my request,
>   that God would grant what I hope for,

that God would be willing to crush me,
    to let loose his hand and cut off my
        life!
Then I would still have this consolation —
    my joy in unrelenting pain —
    that I had not denied the words of the
        Holy One.

"What strength do I have, that I should
        still hope?
    What prospects, that I should be
        patient?
Do I have the strength of stone?
    Is my flesh bronze?
Do I have any power to help myself,
    now that success has been driven
        from me?"

"Do not mortals have hard service on
        earth?
    Are not their days like those of hired
        laborers?
Like a slave longing for the evening
        shadows,
    or a hired laborer waiting to be paid,
so I have been allotted months of
        futility,
    and nights of misery have been
        assigned to me.

When I lie down I think, 'How long before
I get up?'
The night drags on, and I toss and turn
until dawn.
My body is clothed with worms and
scabs,
my skin is broken and festering.

"My days are swifter than a weaver's
shuttle,
and they come to an end without
hope."

SOURCES OF FALSE HOPE

*False hope causes people to plan, build and risk
for something that is not likely to happen. The
Bible identifies several things humans unfortunately place their hope in only to be disappointed in the end.*

False hope ... in riches.

*Because of his fearless confidence in God,
David is able to hurl condemnation at his enemy
who trusts in wealth.*

Why do you boast of evil, you mighty
hero?
Why do you boast all day long,
you who are a disgrace in the eyes
of God?

You who practice deceit,
    your tongue plots destruction;
    it is like a sharpened razor.
You love evil rather than good,
    falsehood rather than speaking the
        truth.
You love every harmful word,
    you deceitful tongue!

Surely God will bring you down to
        everlasting ruin:
    He will snatch you up and pluck you
        from your tent;
    he will uproot you from the land of
        the living.
The righteous will see and fear;
    they will laugh at you, saying,
"Here now is the man
    who did not make God his stronghold
but trusted in his great wealth
    and grew strong by destroying
        others!"

But I am like an olive tree
    flourishing in the house of God;
I trust in God's unfailing love
    for ever and ever.
For what you have done I will always
        praise you
    in the presence of your faithful people.

And I will hope in your name,
for your name is good.

Paul tells Timothy to instruct the believers in Ephesus about the false hope of trusting in riches.

Command those who are rich in this present world not to be arrogant nor to put their hope in wealth, which is so uncertain, but to put their hope in God, who richly provides us with everything for our enjoyment.

False hope ... in people.
The psalmists tell us that we will be disappointed if we place our hope in people rather than God.

It is better to take refuge in the LORD
than to trust in humans.
It is better to take refuge in the LORD
than to trust in princes.

Do not put your trust in princes,
in human beings, who cannot save.
When their spirit departs, they return to
the ground;
on that very day their plans come to
nothing.

The prophet Jeremiah declares the same sentiment.

This is what the LORD says:

> "Cursed is the one who trusts in man,
>   who draws strength from mere
>   flesh
>   and whose heart turns away from
>   the LORD.
> That person will be like a bush in the
>   wastelands;
>   they will not see prosperity when it
>   comes.
> They will dwell in the parched places of
>   the desert,
>   in a salt land where no one lives.

False hope ... in idols
    An idol is any object we place above God.
The prophet Habakkuk declares how foolish it is
to place our hope in such man-made inventions.

> "Of what value is an idol carved by a
>   craftsman?
>   Or an image that teaches lies?
> For the one who makes it trusts in his
>   own creation;
>   he makes idols that cannot speak.

Woe to him who says to wood, 'Come
to life!'
Or to lifeless stone, 'Wake up!'
Can it give guidance?
It is covered with gold and silver;
there is no breath in it."

False hope ... in human government
It is easy and often more tangible for people
to place their trust and hope in nations. Isaiah
warns the people of Judah to avoid such a mis-
take, even with the mighty nation of Egypt.

Woe to those who go down to Egypt
for help,
who rely on horses,
who trust in the multitude of their
chariots
and in the great strength of their
horsemen,
but do not look to the Holy One of Israel,
or seek help from the LORD.

But the Egyptians are mere mortals and
not God;
their horses are flesh and not spirit.
When the LORD stretches out his hand,
those who help will stumble,
those who are helped will fall;
all will perish together.

THE SOURCE OF TRUE HOPE

True hope is found only in God.

Hope is only as good as the power and character of the one who offers it. The psalmist expresses with deep passion his trust in God for his source of hope when present times are tough.

As the deer pants for streams of water,
    so my soul pants for you, my God.
My soul thirsts for God, for the living God.
    When can I go and meet with God?
My tears have been my food
    day and night,
while people say to me all day long,
    "Where is your God?"
These things I remember
    as I pour out my soul:
how I used to go to the house of God
    under the protection of the Mighty One
with shouts of joy and praise
    among the festive throng.

Why, my soul, are you downcast?
    Why so disturbed within me?
Put your hope in God,
    for I will yet praise him,
    my Savior and my God.

My soul is downcast within me;
    therefore I will remember you

from the land of the Jordan,
 the heights of Hermon — from Mount
  Mizar.
Deep calls to deep
 in the roar of your waterfalls;
all your waves and breakers
 have swept over me.

By day the LORD directs his love,
 at night his song is with me —
 a prayer to the God of my life.

I say to God my Rock,
 "Why have you forgotten me?
Why must I go about mourning,
 oppressed by the enemy?"
My bones suffer mortal agony
 as my foes taunt me,
saying to me all day long,
 "Where is your God?"

Why, my soul, are you downcast?
 Why so disturbed within me?
Put your hope in God,
 for I will yet praise him,
 my Savior and my God.

True hope is found in God's promises.

 All the authors of the New Testament wrote on the topic of hope. It is clearly one of the unique and powerful benefits of following God.

The writer of Hebrews drew on the character of God to confirm God's promises.

When God made his promise to Abraham, since there was no one greater for him to swear by, he swore by himself, saying, "I will surely bless you and give you many descendants." And so after waiting patiently, Abraham received what was promised.

People swear by someone greater than themselves, and the oath confirms what is said and puts an end to all argument. Because God wanted to make the unchanging nature of his purpose very clear to the heirs of what was promised, he confirmed it with an oath. God did this so that, by two unchangeable things in which it is impossible for God to lie, we who have fled to take hold of the hope set before us may be greatly encouraged. We have this hope as an anchor for the soul, firm and secure. It enters the inner sanctuary behind the curtain, where our forerunner, Jesus, has entered on our behalf. He has become a high priest forever, in the order of Melchizedek.

Since God's character is rock solid, trustworthy and true, we anchor our hope in his promises to us. Paul wrote a letter to the church at Colossae while he was under house arrest in Rome. God had been unfolding his grand promise of redemption since the fall of Adam and Eve. The true and full content of this promise was a mystery to the people of the Old Testament era. Now, God has fulfilled his promise and revealed it to us—the source of our hope has come.

Now I rejoice in what I am suffering for you, and I fill up in my flesh what is still lacking in regard to Christ's afflictions, for the sake of his body, which is the church. I have become its servant by the commission God gave me to present to you the word of God in its fullness — the mystery that has been kept hidden for ages and generations, but is now disclosed to the Lord's people. To them God has chosen to make known among the Gentiles the glorious riches of this mystery, which is Christ in you, the hope of glory.

He is the one we proclaim, admonishing and teaching everyone with all wisdom, so that we may present everyone fully mature in Christ. To this end I strenuously contend with all the energy Christ so powerfully works in me.

What God has promised to all believers in Jesus enables us to endure the hardships of life. Peter opened his first letter proclaiming this truth. The ultimate promise of God is our future resurrection. The hope of this promise trumps all momentary trials.

Peter, an apostle of Jesus Christ,

To God's elect, exiles scattered throughout the provinces of Pontus, Galatia, Cappadocia, Asia and Bithynia, who have been chosen according to the foreknowledge of God the Father, through the sanctifying work of the Spirit, to be obedient to Jesus Christ and sprinkled with his blood:

Grace and peace be yours in abundance.

Praise be to the God and Father of our Lord Jesus Christ! In his great mercy he has given us new birth into a living hope through the resurrection of Jesus Christ from the dead, and into an inheritance that can never perish, spoil or fade. This inheritance is kept in heaven for you, who through faith are shielded by God's power until the coming of the salvation that is ready to be revealed in the last time. In all this you greatly rejoice, though now for a little while you may have had to suffer grief in all kinds of trials. These have come so that the proven genuineness of your faith — of greater worth than gold, which perishes even though refined by fire — may result in praise, glory and honor when Jesus Christ is revealed. Though you have not seen him, you love him; and even though you do not see him now, you believe in him and are filled with an inexpressible and glorious joy, for you are receiving the end result of your faith, the salvation of your souls.

Concerning this salvation, the prophets, who spoke of the grace that was to come to you, searched intently and with the greatest care, trying to find out the time and circumstances to which the Spirit of Christ in them was pointing when he predicted the sufferings of the Messiah and the glories that would follow. It was revealed to them that they were not serving themselves but you, when they spoke of the things that have now been told you by those who have preached the gospel to you by the Holy Spirit sent from heaven. Even angels long to look into these things.

Therefore, with minds that are alert and fully sober, set your hope on the grace to be brought to you when Jesus Christ is revealed at his coming. As obedient children, do not conform to the evil desires you had when you lived in ignorance. But just as he who called you is holy, so be holy in all you do; for it is written: "Be holy, because I am holy."

Since you call on a Father who judges each person's work impartially, live out your time as foreigners here in reverent fear. For you know that it was not with perishable things such as silver or gold that you were redeemed from the empty way of life handed down to you from your ancestors, but with the precious blood of Christ, a lamb without blemish or defect. He was chosen before the creation of the world, but was revealed in these last times for your sake. Through him you believe in God, who raised him from the dead and glorified him, and so your faith and hope are in God.

Now that you have purified yourselves by obeying the truth so that you have sincere love for each other, love one another deeply, from the heart. For you have been born again, not of perishable seed, but of imperishable, through the living and enduring word of God. For,

> "All people are like grass,
>   and all their glory is like the flowers of
>   the field;
> the grass withers and the flowers fall,
>   but the word of the Lord endures
>   forever."

And this is the word that was preached to you.

The Christians in Thessalonica had misunderstood Paul and thought that all believers would live until Christ returns. That caused them distress when some in the church died. Paul wrote his first letter to them to clear up this matter. The promise to all believers, past and present, of being with the Lord forever is the foundation of our hope.

Brothers and sisters, we do not want you to be uninformed about those who sleep in death, so that you do not grieve like the rest of mankind, who have no hope. For we believe that Jesus died and rose again, and so we believe that God will bring with Jesus those who have fallen asleep in him. According to the Lord's word, we tell you that we who are still alive, who are left until the coming of the Lord, will certainly not precede those who have fallen asleep. For the Lord himself will come down from heaven, with a loud command, with the voice of the archangel and with the trumpet call of God, and the dead in Christ will rise first. After that, we who are still alive and are left will be caught up together with them in the clouds to meet the Lord in the air. And so we will be with the Lord forever. Therefore encourage one another with these words.

John echoed the writings of Paul and Peter regarding the hope we have through the promised resurrection. He challenged his readers to live pure lives in anticipation of this guaranteed event.

See what great love the Father has lavished on us, that we should be called children of God! And that is what we are! The reason the world does not know us is that it did not know him. Dear friends, now we are children of God, and what we will be has not yet been made known. But we know that when Christ appears, we shall be like him, for we shall see him as he is. All who have this hope in him purify themselves, just as he is pure.

THE EFFECT OF HOPE

God and his promises are the reason for our hope. When we embrace this hope, it has a dramatic effect on our daily lives. Hope gives us the ability to get through our days, to persevere. Simeon waited many long years without seeing the fulfillment of his hope, but he carried on, letting hope give him strength for each new day.

Now there was a man in Jerusalem called Simeon, who was righteous and devout. He was waiting for the consolation of Israel, and the Holy Spirit was on him. It had been revealed to him by the Holy Spirit that he would not die before he had seen the Lord's Messiah. Moved by the Spirit, he went into the temple courts. When the parents brought in the child Jesus to do for him what the custom of the Law required, Simeon took him in his arms and praised God, saying:

> "Sovereign Lord, as you have promised,
>   you may now dismiss your servant in
>   peace.
> For my eyes have seen your salvation,
>   which you have prepared in the sight of
>   all nations:

a light for revelation to the Gentiles,
  and the glory of your people Israel."

The child's father and mother marveled at what was said about him. Then Simeon blessed them and said to Mary, his mother: "This child is destined to cause the falling and rising of many in Israel, and to be a sign that will be spoken against, so that the thoughts of many hearts will be revealed. And a sword will pierce your own soul too."

Isaiah prophesied about the coming captivity of the people of Judah by the Babylonians. This portion of the book of Isaiah looks beyond that and assumes the 70 years of exile are almost over. Isaiah was able to encourage the people with confidence because he based his hope in God and his promise to bring the people home. The exiles could live full, happy lives because they knew God would keep his promise.

Comfort, comfort my people,
  says your God.
Speak tenderly to Jerusalem,
  and proclaim to her
that her hard service has been completed,
  that her sin has been paid for,
that she has received from the LORD's
    hand
  double for all her sins.

A voice of one calling:
"In the wilderness prepare
    the way for the LORD;
make straight in the desert
    a highway for our God.
Every valley shall be raised up,
    every mountain and hill made low;
the rough ground shall become level,
    the rugged places a plain.
And the glory of the LORD will be
        revealed,
        and all people will see it together.
                For the mouth of the LORD
                    has spoken."

A voice says, "Cry out."
    And I said, "What shall I cry?"

"All people are like grass,
    and all their faithfulness is like the
        flowers of the field.
The grass withers and the flowers fall,
    because the breath of the LORD blows
        on them.
    Surely the people are grass.
The grass withers and the flowers fall,
    but the word of our God endures
        forever."

You who bring good news to Zion,
    go up on a high mountain.

You who bring good news to Jerusalem,
    lift up your voice with a shout,
lift it up, do not be afraid;
    say to the towns of Judah,
    "Here is your God!"
See, the Sovereign LORD comes with
        power,
    and he rules with a mighty arm.
See, his reward is with him,
    and his recompense accompanies him.
He tends his flock like a shepherd:
    He gathers the lambs in his arms
and carries them close to his heart;
    he gently leads those that have young.

Who has measured the waters in the
        hollow of his hand,
    or with the breadth of his hand marked
        off the heavens?
Who has held the dust of the earth in a
        basket,
    or weighed the mountains on the
        scales
    and the hills in a balance?
Who can fathom the Spirit of the LORD,
    or instruct the LORD as his counselor?
Whom did the LORD consult to enlighten
        him,
    and who taught him the right way?

Who was it that taught him knowledge,
    or showed him the path of
        understanding?

Surely the nations are like a drop in a
        bucket;
    they are regarded as dust on the scales;
    he weighs the islands as though they
        were fine dust.
Lebanon is not sufficient for altar fires,
    nor its animals enough for burnt
        offerings.
Before him all the nations are as nothing;
    they are regarded by him as worthless
    and less than nothing.

With whom, then, will you compare
        God?
    To what image will you liken him?
As for an idol, a metalworker casts it,
    and a goldsmith overlays it with gold
    and fashions silver chains for it.
A person too poor to present such an
        offering
    selects wood that will not rot;
they look for a skilled worker
    to set up an idol that will not topple.

Do you not know?
    Have you not heard?

Has it not been told you from the
      beginning?
   Have you not understood since the
      earth was founded?
He sits enthroned above the circle of the
      earth,
   and its people are like grasshoppers.
He stretches out the heavens like a
      canopy,
   and spreads them out like a tent to
      live in.
He brings princes to naught
   and reduces the rulers of this world to
      nothing.
No sooner are they planted,
   no sooner are they sown,
   no sooner do they take root in the
      ground,
than he blows on them and they wither,
   and a whirlwind sweeps them away like
      chaff.

"To whom will you compare me?
   Or who is my equal?" says the Holy One.
Lift up your eyes and look to the heavens:
   Who created all these?
He who brings out the starry host one
      by one
   and calls forth each of them by name.

Because of his great power and mighty
        strength,
    not one of them is missing.

Why do you complain, Jacob?
    Why do you say, Israel,
"My way is hidden from the LORD;
    my cause is disregarded by my God"?
Do you not know?
    Have you not heard?
The LORD is the everlasting God,
    the Creator of the ends of the earth.
He will not grow tired or weary,
    and his understanding no one can
        fathom.
He gives strength to the weary
    and increases the power of the weak.
Even youths grow tired and weary,
    and young men stumble and fall;
but those who hope in the LORD
    will renew their strength.
They will soar on wings like eagles;
    they will run and not grow weary,
    they will walk and not be faint.

About a century after Isaiah died, his prediction of the Babylonian captivity was fulfilled during the lifetime of the prophet Jeremiah. Jeremiah's message to God's people was similar to Isaiah's:

*Although the people were captive, God's prom-
ises could give them hope for their daily living.
And he offers that same hope to Christians
today.*

This is the text of the letter that the prophet Jeremiah sent from Jerusalem to the surviv-
ing elders among the exiles and to the priests,
the prophets and all the other people Nebuchadnezzar had carried into exile from Jerusalem to
Babylon. (This was after King Jehoiachin and the
queen mother, the court officials and the leaders
of Judah and Jerusalem, the skilled workers and
the artisans had gone into exile from Jerusalem.)
He entrusted the letter to Elasah son of Shaphan
and to Gemariah son of Hilkiah, whom Zedeki-
ah king of Judah sent to King Nebuchadnezzar in
Babylon. It said:

This is what the LORD Almighty, the God of
Israel, says to all those I carried into exile from
Jerusalem to Babylon: "Build houses and settle
down; plant gardens and eat what they produce.
Marry and have sons and daughters; find wives
for your sons and give your daughters in mar-
riage, so that they too may have sons and daughters. Increase in number there; do not decrease.
Also, seek the peace and prosperity of the city to
which I have carried you into exile. Pray to the

LORD for it, because if it prospers, you too will prosper." Yes, this is what the LORD Almighty, the God of Israel, says: "Do not let the prophets and diviners among you deceive you. Do not listen to the dreams you encourage them to have. They are prophesying lies to you in my name. I have not sent them," declares the LORD.

This is what the LORD says: "When seventy years are completed for Babylon, I will come to you and fulfill my good promise to bring you back to this place. For I know the plans I have for you," declares the LORD, "plans to prosper you and not to harm you, plans to give you hope and a future."

HOPE ACTIVATES FAITH, FAITH DEEPENS HOPE

Hope is available to all followers of God, but not everyone takes hold of it. It can be hard for us to trust in a God we cannot see and hold fast to fantastic promises yet to come. To activate the power of hope in our lives, we need to have faith in God and his promises. The writer of Hebrews preached this message to his readers. He then listed people from the past who placed their faith in God and experienced amazing results in their lives. God offers this same opportunity to us today. In fact, God has "something better" planned for those who know Jesus.

Now faith is confidence in what we hope for and assurance about what we do not see. This is what the ancients were commended for.

By faith we understand that the universe was formed at God's command, so that what is seen was not made out of what was visible.

By faith Abel brought God a better offering than Cain did. By faith he was commended as righteous, when God spoke well of his offerings. And by faith Abel still speaks, even though he is dead.

By faith Enoch was taken from this life, so that he did not experience death: "He could not be found, because God had taken him away." For before he was taken, he was commended as one who pleased God. And without faith it is impossible to please God, because anyone who comes to him must believe that he exists and that he rewards those who earnestly seek him.

By faith Noah, when warned about things not yet seen, in holy fear built an ark to save his family. By his faith he condemned the world and became heir of the righteousness that is in keeping with faith.

By faith Abraham, when called to go to a place he would later receive as his inheritance, obeyed and went, even though he did not know where he was going. By faith he made his home in the promised land like a stranger in a foreign country; he lived in tents, as did Isaac and Jacob, who were heirs with him of the same promise. For he was looking forward to the city with foundations, whose architect and builder is God. And by faith even Sarah, who was past childbearing age, was enabled to bear children because she considered him faithful who had made the promise. And so from this one man, and he as good as dead, came descendants as numerous as the stars in the sky and as countless as the sand on the seashore.

All these people were still living by faith when they died. They did not receive the things promised; they only saw them and welcomed them from a distance, admitting that they were foreigners and strangers on earth. People who say such things show that they are looking for a country of their own. If they had been thinking of the country they had left, they would have had opportunity to return. Instead, they were longing for a better country — a heavenly one. Therefore God is not ashamed to be called their God, for he has prepared a city for them.

By faith Abraham, when God tested him, offered Isaac as a sacrifice. He who had embraced the promises was about to sacrifice his one and only son, even though God had said to him, "It is through Isaac that your offspring will be reckoned." Abraham reasoned that God could even raise the dead, and so in a manner of speaking he did receive Isaac back from death.

By faith Isaac blessed Jacob and Esau in regard to their future.

By faith Jacob, when he was dying, blessed each of Joseph's sons, and worshiped as he leaned on the top of his staff.

By faith Joseph, when his end was near, spoke about the exodus of the Israelites from Egypt and gave instructions concerning the burial of his bones.

By faith Moses' parents hid him for three months after he was born, because they saw he was no ordinary child, and they were not afraid of the king's edict.

By faith Moses, when he had grown up, refused to be known as the son of Pharaoh's daughter. He chose to be mistreated along with the people of God rather than to enjoy the fleeting pleasures of sin. He regarded disgrace for the sake of Christ as of greater value than the treasures of Egypt, because he was looking ahead to his reward. By faith he left Egypt, not fearing the king's anger; he persevered because he saw him who is invisible. By faith he kept the Passover and the application of blood, so that the destroyer of the firstborn would not touch the firstborn of Israel.

By faith the people passed through the Red

Sea as on dry land; but when the Egyptians tried to do so, they were drowned.

By faith the walls of Jericho fell, after the army had marched around them for seven days.

By faith the prostitute Rahab, because she welcomed the spies, was not killed with those who were disobedient.

And what more shall I say? I do not have time to tell about Gideon, Barak, Samson and Jephthah, about David and Samuel and the prophets, who through faith conquered kingdoms, administered justice, and gained what was promised; who shut the mouths of lions, quenched the fury of the flames, and escaped the edge of the sword; whose weakness was turned to strength; and who became powerful in battle and routed foreign armies. Women received back their dead, raised to life again. There were others who were tortured, refusing to be released so that they might gain an even better resurrection. Some faced jeers and flogging, and even chains and imprisonment. They were put to death by stoning; they were sawed in two; they were killed by the sword. They went about in sheepskins and goatskins, destitute, persecuted and mistreated — the world was not worthy of them. They wandered in deserts and mountains, living in caves and in holes in the ground.

These were all commended for their faith, yet

none of them received what had been promised, since God had planned something better for us so that only together with us would they be made perfect.

Therefore, since we are surrounded by such a great cloud of witnesses, let us throw off everything that hinders and the sin that so easily entangles. And let us run with perseverance the race marked out for us, fixing our eyes on Jesus, the pioneer and perfecter of faith. For the joy set before him he endured the cross, scorning its shame, and sat down at the right hand of the throne of God. Consider him who endured such opposition from sinners, so that you will not grow weary and lose heart.

Chart of References

CHAPTER 1: ETERNITY

2 Kings 2:1–18
Luke 16:19–31
1 Corinthians 15:1–28, 35–58
2 Corinthians 4:13—5:10

1 Thessalonians 4:13—5:11
2 Peter 3:1–18
Revelation 20:11—22:21
John 14:1–7

CHAPTER 2: SINGLE-MINDEDNESS

Exodus 20:2–3
Deuteronomy 6:1–9
Matthew 6:19–33
Philippians 3:1–14
2 Chronicles 20:1–30
John 8:12–30

Matthew 14:22–36
Acts 5:12–42
Deuteronomy 29:16—30:20
Romans 12:1–2
Colossians 3:1–4
Colossians 3:15–17

CHAPTER 3: HOPE

Job 6:1–13
Job 7:1–6
Psalm 52:1–9
1 Timothy 6:17
Psalm 118:8–9
Psalm 146:3–4
Jeremiah 17:5–6
Habakkuk 2:18–19
Isaiah 31:1,3
Psalm 42:1–11

Hebrews 6:13–20
Colossians 1:24–29
1 Peter 1:1–25
1 Thessalonians 4:13–18
1 John 3:1–3
Luke 2:25–35
Isaiah 40:1–31
Jeremiah 29:1–11
Hebrews 11:1—12:3

BELIEVE

POWERED BY ZONDERVAN

Dear Reader,

Notable researcher George Gallup Jr. summarized his findings on the state of American Christianity with this startling revelation: **"The stark fact is, many Christians don't know what they believe or why."**

The problem is not that people lack a hunger for God's Word. Research tells us that the number one thing people want from their church is for it to help them understand the Bible, and that Bible engagement is the number one catalyst for spiritual growth. Nothing else comes close.

This is why I am passionate about *Believe*—a Bible engagement experience to anchor every member of your family in the key teachings of the Bible.

Grounded in Scripture, *Believe* is a spiritual growth experience that helps people of all ages become more like Jesus in their beliefs, actions, and character.

When these timeless truths are understood, believed in the heart, and applied to our daily living, they can transform a life, a family, a church, a city, a nation, and even our world.

Imagine thousands of churches and countless individuals all over the world finally able to declare—**"I know what I believe and why, and in God's strength I will seek to live it out all the days of my life."**

It could change the world.

In Him,

Randy Frazee
General Editor, *Believe*

LIVING THE STORY OF THE BIBLE TO BECOME LIKE JESUS

Teach your whole family how to think, act, and be like Jesus!

- **Adults** – Unlocks the 10 key beliefs, 10 key practices, and 10 key virtues of a Christian. Curriculum also available.
- *Think, Act, Be Like Jesus* – This companion to *Believe* helps readers develop a personal vision and a simple plan for getting started on their spiritual growth journey.
- **Students** – Contains the same Scriptures as the adult edition, but with transitions and fun features to engage students. Curriculum also available.
- **Children** – With a Kids' Edition for ages 8-12, a Storybook for ages 4-8, and three levels of curriculum, children of all ages will learn how to think, act, and be like Jesus.
- **Churches** – *Believe* is flexible, affordable, and easy to use with your church, in any ministry, from nursery to adults...and even the whole church.
- **Spanish** – All *Believe* resources are also available in Spanish.

FOR ADULTS

9780310433583   9780310250173

FOR STUDENTS

9780310745617

FOR CHILDREN

9780310746010   9780310745907

FOR CHURCHES

Campaign Kit 9780310681717

WHAT YOU BELIEVE DRIVES EVERYTHING.

Grounded in Scripture, *Believe* is a topical abridgment of the NIV Bible, unlocking the 10 key beliefs, 10 key practices, and 10 key virtues that will help you become more like Jesus in your beliefs, actions, and character.

Learn the core truths of the Christian faith and how to live them out all the days of your life.

Know What You Believe and Why It Matters.

Hardcover   9780310433583

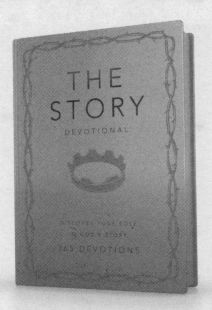

THE STORY DEVOTIONAL
Discover Your Role in God's Story

See your life and purpose in a whole new light—as part of God's epic story—with this beautiful leather-look devotional. Through 365 daily Scripture readings arranged chronologically, plus bite-sized reflections and a daily takeaway, this unique devotional illuminates how God has been weaving his plan throughout history. Each day, you'll be blessed with a reminder of God's unrelenting love and pursuit of his people.

Tan Leathersoft   9780310341895

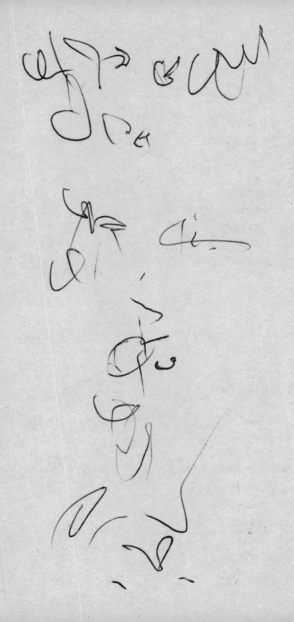